IMAGES
of America

THE ANTHRACITE COAL
REGION'S SLAVIC COMMUNITY

On the cover: Choirs such as this group from Northumberland County in 1923 once filled churches and parish halls throughout the entire anthracite coal region. Dressed in elaborately detailed national costume, Slavic choral groups sang a repertoire of liturgical hymns in languages brought from the homelands by the original immigrants. (Transfiguration Ukrainian Greek Catholic Church, Shamokin.)

IMAGES
of America

THE ANTHRACITE COAL REGION'S SLAVIC COMMUNITY

Brian Ardan

ARCADIA
PUBLISHING

Published by Arcadia Publishing
Charleston, South Carolina

Library of Congress Catalog Card Number: 2008928787

For all general information contact Arcadia Publishing at:
Telephone 843-853-2070
Fax 843-853-0044
E-mail sales@arcadiapublishing.com
For customer service and orders:
Toll-Free 1-888-313-2665

Visit us on the Internet at www.arcadiapublishing.com

CONTENTS

ACKNOWLEDGMENTS

In taking on this project, I discovered quickly the large amount of time, effort, and support that would be needed to complete the job. As I look back on the past eight months and myriad trips throughout the anthracite coal region, I am certain that this book would never have made it to the publisher without the generous help of those people and organizations listed below.

I would, therefore, like to extend my gratitude, in no particular order, to the clergy and staff at all the contributing churches, the Area Polish Cultural Club, the Sisters of SS. Cyril and Methodius in Danville, Fr. Mark Fesniak, John Kameen and the Forest City News, the Iskra family, Ewa Ostasz at the St. Vladimir Foundation in Krakow, Poland, the Muzeum Etnograficzne im. Seweryna Udzieli w Krakowie, Anne Trauger, John Orsulak, the Nanticoke Historical Society, Cindy Inkrote, the Northumberland County Historical Society, the Polish Falcons in Mocanaqua, Dr. Peter Yasenchak, the Historical Society of Schuylkill County, Eric Smith, the Znaniecki family and the ladies from the Polish Room at Wilkes University, Andrew Chuba, Barbara Puchnick, Emil Simodejka, John Kelnock, Rose Demsko, Amy Johnson, Msgr. Stephen Hrynuck, the Polish National Catholic Church, the fraternal and beneficial societies that donated materials, and all the individuals and families contributing photographs and documents from their personal collections.

I also owe a great debt of thanks to Dr. Tara L. Fulton, dean of library and information services at Lock Haven University of Pennsylvania, without whose support this project likely would not have happened. To all my friends and colleagues at Lock Haven University, I thank you for your encouragement and patience. I also thank, as usual, Monique LaRocque and David Libby for being such loyal and lifelong friends. Finally, I would especially like to thank my family. We have been through an awful lot together this year, and I love you all the more.

INTRODUCTION

The history of Pennsylvania's anthracite coal region could not be told accurately without the inclusion of Slavic people. In the latter half of the 19th century, individuals identifying themselves as Poles, Slovaks, Rusyns, Ukrainians, and others began what would become a steady stream of immigration lasting well into the 20th century. While seeking cheap labor to work in the anthracite veins, as well as in the factories that sprung up around the mines, the bosses of big business recruited Slavs heavily from areas such as the Carpathian Mountains and other economically depressed European regions. Viewed by mine owners as low-cost, abundant, and expendable labor, these new workers appeared to constitute perfect tools for building empires from the black seams buried deep inside area mountains.

When the Slavs arrived, ethnic groups that had been longer established in the region often viewed them as an unwelcome and dangerous threat. Not only were they seen as harmful to employment and job security, they also brought with them a culture quite foreign to the status quo. Although deeply religious, their practices often roamed far afield of anything previously witnessed in the region. In addition, they frequently reveled in raucous celebrations fortified by bathtub whiskey and other homemade brews. Weddings went on for days. Funerals did much the same, all to the tune of music that had a decidedly non-western timbre. It is no surprise, then, that many Slavs met with resistance, and at times violence, on the part of United States–born citizens who coined pejorative phrases such as "Hunky" and "Greenhorn" in reference to the unwanted arrivals.

In one sense, the early rejection by longer-established groups hindered Slavic integration into the mainstream. In another, however, anti-Slav sentiment forced the immigrants to focus efforts on group—and intergroup—activities aimed at unity and cultural preservation. Early immigrants quickly began establishing their own religious and secular organizations, including a large number of ethnic parishes. With time, they also managed to send for families back home, purchase a house, and carve out their own niche in the recently adopted nation. In the process, they began cultivating a unique Slavic American character shaped by New World experience and Old World heritage.

As the decades passed, Slavs continuously maintained and developed their identity. They also, however, integrated into local culture and in turn found themselves accepted by those around them. Once they had successfully entered the mainstream as Slavic Americans, they began to help chart its path. As a result, they steadily placed a distinctive mark on local, regional, and even national culture. Numerous anthracite immigrants and their descendants, for example, have gone on to achieve recognition in a variety of areas. Among them are noted telegraphy pioneer and priest Jozef Murgaš; Hollywood screenwriter and director Joseph L. Mankiewicz, winner of four Academy Awards; baseball hall of famer Stanley Coveleski; actor Jack Palance; *New York Times* best-selling author and ex–Navy SEAL Richard Marcinko; and more. Ultimately, the Slavic American presence in the region developed into a distinct and cohesive identity that is still tangible up to the present, long after the once powerful mining industry that drew it here has declined and, in most places, disappeared.

Today the Slavic identity in anthracite asserts itself in nearly every town from Shamokin to Carbondale. Eastern Rite churches adorned with golden "onion top" domes tower above city streets with stores bearing names like Kowalonek's Kielbasy Shop in Shenandoah, featuring Polish sausage and other Slavic delicacies. Ethnically related drinking establishments, as well as social and fraternal organizations, can still be found in anthracite towns: the Polish Falcons in Mocanaqua and the Area Polish Cultural Club in Mount Carmel to name a few. Various seasonal activities such as classes on *pysanky* painting attest to the enduring Slavic heritage in the region. In addition, church festivals continue to have a decidedly ethnic feel, with many offering foods such as pierogi, *halushki, halupki, bigos*, and more. The church-supported Ukrainian Seminary Day, for example, comprises a highly anticipated annual festival for many in the Minersville area. Here local and regional music groups such as the 51-year-old Original Byzantine Men's Choir perform throughout the day. Polkas bands play a mixture of English- and Slavic-language tunes, couples dance, and vendors sell their wares, all within shouting distance of the ever-present beer stand hawking the favorite local lager.

As for the region itself, the anthracite landscape unfortunately continues to bear the environmental scars of both deep and strip mining. Numerous streams run orange with acidic drainage, and abandoned mine sites dot the landscape. Other industries, such as the cigar factories and silk mills that once relied on a workforce consisting of miners' wives and daughters, have long moved on, leaving forsaken structures as empty reminders of the area's golden age. Nevertheless, the region continues to survive, and in places thrive, despite the realities of economic hard times and brain drain that have for years taken many local youths to more promising locales such as Philadelphia and Baltimore. The area survives because of the tenacity of its long-term residents. Like the early Slavic settlers, they maintain a strong work ethic bolstered by deeply rooted connections to family and their immediate physical environment. Many people of the area feel so tied to this region and its culture that living in another place is simply out of the question. Those who have left seem invariably to carry their identity as a former "coal cracker" like a unique badge of honor, a sense of belonging to a club whose membership is inherited through birth in the region and lasts for life.

After the mines went into irreversible decline, it seemed like the area would never recover. However, in recent years, certain industries have moved into the region, attracted by a ready workforce and cheap land costs. The proximity to larger markets such as New York City and Philadelphia also makes the area appealing to potential investors. Finally, an unforeseen boost to the local economy has been the growth of the tourism industry. The anthracite area, for example, has been able to capitalize successfully on its former industrial past by setting up history-related tourist attractions such as the Steamtown National Historic Site in Scranton, Eckley Miners' Village near Hazleton, and the Ashland Mine Tour. Knoebels Amusement Resort in Elysburg packs tens of thousands of tourists into the park each summer. Many of those same tourists take the time to visit the mining exhibit on the grounds and pick up a few souvenirs along the way. The town of Jim Thorpe, also known as Mauch Chunk, draws thousands of day-trippers who hike trails and navigate waters surrounding this former coal producer in the anthracite Southern field.

In general, the region is an area deeply rooted in its ethnic and industrial past, with increasing signs of a promising future. As times change, however, one thing remains constant: a determined group of people who view their hometowns and history with a great deal of pride. Among them are the descendants of Slavic nations in southern, eastern, and central Europe. Their story, documented in the vintage photographs of this text, constitutes an important vehicle for capturing one aspect of what it means to be a modern-day Slav hailing from the anthracite coal region.

Before proceeding, it might be helpful to clarify what is meant by the phrase *Slavic* and to identify more precisely those groups comprising the focus of this book. In brief, Slavs are a group of people with ancestral roots posited to be in eastern Europe. Many centuries ago, Slavic tribes conducted a series of migrations to various locations on the European continent, including present-day Russia and Ukraine in the east and as far south as the Balkan Peninsula. In terms of religious affiliation, Slavs typically adhere to Eastern Christianity or Catholicism. Additionally, some smaller groups follow the teachings of Judaism, Protestantism, and Islam. Their languages are a part of the Indo-European group and fall into one of three categories: East Slavic (Ukrainians, Russians, and Belarusians), West Slavic (Slovaks, Czechs, Poles, and Sorbs), and South Slavic (Serbs, Croats, Bosniaks, Montenegrins, Slovenes, Bulgarians, and Macedonians).

To a certain extent, the taxonomy above may be considered incomplete, as it does not take into account ethnic and linguistic subgroupings or the tendency of some smaller populations to identify themselves as distinct from neighboring groups. One classic example—and quite relevant for the purposes of the current text—concerns the Carpatho-Rusyns (Ruthenians, Ruthenes, Rusnaks, Rusins, and colloquial misnomer "Russians"), a Slavic group that once immigrated in great numbers to the anthracite region. Frequently classified as Ukrainian, many Carpatho-Rusyns historically have cited a linguistic, cultural, and experiential heritage that defines them as separate from their neighbors to the east. Ukrainian advocates, on the other hand, claim that Carpatho-Rusyns are ethnically Ukrainian and vigorously downplay any notions of separateness. To say the least, disputes such as this—often taking place over many decades and sometimes on more than one continent—make classification a less-than-exact endeavor that invariably fails to satisfy all those named under a given rubric. Regarding the Ukrainian/Carpatho-Rusyn question, the present text avoids polemics. If, for example, an organization seen on a photograph in the book identified itself as Rusyn during one period, and later as Ukrainian, the author cites the name employed by the organization at the time the photograph was taken, or the name written on the original image. In this manner, the book minimizes points of contention, choosing instead to concentrate on commonalities that define, unite, and celebrate the history of Slavs in the region.

Although individuals from numerous Slavic groups noted above came to Pennsylvania to work and establish lives in the New World, the present text focuses on a decidedly narrower list: Slovaks, Poles, Ukrainians, and Carpatho-Rusyns, with restricted coverage given to several other groups. The rationale behind such narrowing of focus is twofold. First, the limited scope of a short, pictorial history precludes comprehensive coverage of all groups entering the coal region. Second, those groups that have been selected provide the largest, most visible and enduring imprint marking the historical presence of Slavs in hard coal country.

So, how does one begin to tell the local story—in 200 or so photographs nonetheless—of a multilingual, multinational group of people set against a backdrop of 150-plus years across a geographic space covering several counties? The task becomes even more difficult when gauging the depth and breadth of religious organizations, social clubs, fraternal societies, ethnically related sports teams, events, and more brought to the table by just one of the groups under consideration. A typical ethnic parish in the region, for example, has customarily maintained numerous men's groups, women's groups, a choir, youth organizations, prayer circles, even theatrical clubs and musical ensembles. With several Slavic parishes often existing in even the smallest of coal towns, the number of organizations and activities multiplies greatly when taking into consideration all groups across the region, to a point where in-depth coverage becomes unfeasible in a brief, image-driven work. *The Anthracite Coal Region's Slavic Community*, therefore, does not attempt to identify each Slavic organization and activity extant in the area. Rather, it employs a broad-stroke approach; individual photographs obtained from around the region illustrate those aspects of Slavic life universally experienced in anthracite locales. Thematically the pictures cover topics that have informed and shaped Slavic identity, including the Old

9

World; early immigration; adapting to the new land; life in and around the mines; the growth of churches and religious life; and culture, tradition, heritage, and customs. Collectively, the photographs and captions help create a picture, albeit broad, of the history and cultural legacy of Slavic people in the anthracite coal region.

Throughout the book, quotes are drawn from several academic texts found in the paragraph below. However, many of the dates, names, and other factual material presented in the captions accompanying the photographs come from a variety of unpublished sources. These include handwritten notes on the back of the original photographs, parish jubilee books, letters, and ephemera, as well as in-person interviews. They do not appear in the following list. For more information on these sources, please contact the author via Arcadia Publishing.

Readers interested in learning more about coal mining and/or Slavic people in the anthracite region may wish to begin with the following texts and articles: "Polish Miners in Luzerne County Pennsylvania" in the journal *Polish American Studies* (1946) by Sr. M. Bern Accursia, *Anthracite People: Families, Unions and Work 1900–1940* (1983) by John Bodnar, *The Poems of Anton Piotrowski* (1998) by Harold E. Cox, *The Slavic Community on Strike: Immigrant Labor in Pennsylvania Anthracite* (1968) by Victor R. Greene, *Minstrels of the Mine Patch: Songs and Stories of the Anthracite Industry* (1938) by George Korson, and *The Kingdom of Coal: Work, Enterprise, and Ethnic Communities in the Mine Fields* (1998) by Donald L. Miller and Richard E. Sharpless.

Children and young adults may be interested in reading *Growing Up in Coal Country* (1996) and *A Coal Miner's Bride: The Diary of Anetka Kaminska, Lattimer, Pennsylvania, 1896* (2003), both authored by Susan Campbell Bartoletti.

One

THE OLD WORLD

In a work aiming to create a collective snapshot of the Slavic experience in the anthracite coal region, it seems fitting to establish first an Old World starting point, for it was in the towns and small hamlets of Slavic Europe that many thousands of future immigrants first entertained any thoughts of life abroad.

In the time preceding the great migration to the anthracite region, a typical Slav found herself or himself in a world that often extended no farther than a distant mountain ridge; where the local church formed an absolute spiritual and social focal point; where, for many, days entailed working on farms or tending to livestock in pastures; and where sunrise and sunset dictated the natural rhythms of life.

By the mid- to late 1800s, however, Slavs had begun experiencing an increasing amount of unrest and discontent. While a variety of reasons likely contributed, unfavorable economic conditions served as arguably the overriding factor prompting most future immigrants to consider moving overseas. In many locations, conditions on rural farmsteads had for years been abominable. With little hope of buying new land, many Slavs worked small family plots that were heavily overused and long depleted of essential nutrients. This overuse, in turn, helped create widespread hunger, squalid living conditions, and an urgent necessity to find practical solutions to long-standing economic woes.

It is in this social and economic framework that the original immigrants to the anthracite coal region began their life-altering journeys. This chapter briefly examines scenes from day-to-day life in various Old World Slavic locations. By viewing faces, homes, churches, work, dress, entertainment, and customs, a picture steadily emerges: a picture not of the famed "huddled masses" but of individuals and their immediate environment. For modern-day Slavs, these pictures offer a glimpse into the daily lives of their forebears. To be sure, a striking contrast exists between 19th-century rural Europe and contemporary life. Nevertheless, a strong and not-too-distant bloodline still connects those Slavs seen in the following pages with their descendants living in the anthracite region.

This first image shows a traditionally dressed Hutsul from Verkhovyna in the Ivano-Frankivsk province of modern-day Ukraine. Hutsuls are a group of Carpathian highlanders, with neighboring populations traditionally including Boykos and Lemkos. Individuals from each of these groups would eventually help comprise the massive immigration to the anthracite coal region. (Muzeum Etnograficzne im. Seweryna Udzieli w Krakowie.)

This photograph shows a married couple in Poland during the latter half of the 19th century. Jan and Maria Hodur were impoverished farmers who raised a family in the town of Zarki. Among their children was Franciszek (Francis) Hodur, who would later go on to found the Polish National Catholic Church in Scranton in 1897. (Polish National Catholic Church.)

A trickle of Slovak immigrants came to America in the 1860s. By 1880, the numbers had risen considerably, with thousands residing in the anthracite coal region. At that time, the majority of Slovaks practiced Roman Catholicism. In their numbers, though, were a fair number of Protestants, Greek Catholics, and Orthodox. The Kapusta family, shown here in Slovakia, poses with rosaries and prayer books in hand. (Iskra family.)

This young couple hailed from the Carpathian Mountains. At the time of the photograph, regional economic conditions made life difficult for those seeking to start their own families. Many couples, therefore, opted to risk their future in a distant place called the anthracite coal region of Pennsylvania. (Muzeum Etnograficzne im. Seweryna Udzieli w Krakowie.)

In addition to the economic problems and antiquated farming methods found in numerous Old World Slavic areas, a large population growth contributed to a worsening of conditions for many. As income failed to keep pace with needs, Slavic families and extended families were forced to survive on increasingly less. (Muzeum Etnograficzne im. Seweryna Udzieli w Krakowie.)

This horse-drawn cart illustrates a typical scene in a Lithuanian village during the time when many eastern, southern, and central Europeans began their long journey to the United States. Although their language does not belong to the Slavic group, Lithuanians share a closely related history and culture with Poland. In the latter half of the 19th century, Poles and Lithuanians alike would begin filling anthracite towns and cities. (Library of Congress, Prints and Photographs Division.)

Like the Poles and Lithuanians, Lemkos would eventually enter the coal region by the many thousands. Lemkos are a mountain people hailing from the Beskid Niski and Bieszczady areas of present-day Poland, as well as from locales to the south in Slovakia. This photograph shows a large group of Lemkos in Wapienne near Gorlice, Poland. (Muzeum Etnograficzne im. Seweryna Udzieli w Krakowie.)

In many ways similar to their Lemko and Hutsul neighbors, Boykos are an ethnic group hailing from the mountains in present-day Ukraine, Poland, and Slovakia. As a rule, most adhere to one of several Eastern Christian religions. To earn a living, many Boyko highlanders traditionally raised white oxen, cattle, and other livestock. This photograph depicts a group of Boykos in their national dress. (Muzeum Etnograficzne im. Seweryna Udzieli w Krakowie; photograph by T. Seweryn.)

As Slavic men began settling into the anthracite region, they often did so alone. Those without wives back home soon found themselves with few opportunities to meet spouses in the new land. Young and eligible women such as those in the photographs on this page, therefore, at times faced the unwelcome prospect of traveling abroad to meet a future husband via a prearranged marriage agreement. (Muzeum Etnograficzne im. Seweryna Udzieli w Krakowie.)

Initially it was common practice for mothers to remain in the old country, tasked with raising children, working the land, and generally tending to family matters while sons and husbands emigrated to work in the mines of the anthracite region. The first photograph shows a woman and two children in Czechoslovakia, 1931, in traditional dress. The second image, from the 1920s, shows a Ukrainian woman and her daughter, also in traditional clothing. While similarities can be found in many forms of Slavic folk dress, individual groups developed unique patterns and styles that characterized a given region or ethnic affiliation. (Right, Jankola Library; below, Muzeum Etnograficzne im. Seweryna Udzieli w Krakowie.)

17

The senior members of Slavic society represented the least likely of all groups to make the transition into the New World. Burgeoning locales such as the anthracite region offered work for individuals who were enterprising, healthy, and, perhaps most essentially, young. In many cases, therefore, the elderly could only watch with compassionate acceptance as sons and daughters departed for the New World. (Muzeum Etnograficzne im. Seweryna Udzieli w Krakowie.)

The process of immigration to the anthracite region from locales in Europe forced families to endure the hardships of separation. Pictured here are two sisters and their niece from Kladzan, Slovakia. While one brother of the sisters remained in the hometown, two others set off at young ages to live permanently in North America. Neither sister ever saw these two brothers again after they left for the United States. (Anne Trauger.)

Although extreme poverty characterized many towns and hamlets in eastern and central Europe near the dawn of the 20th century, local residents traditionally pooled their meager earnings to build, adorn, and maintain surprisingly elaborate parishes. This Eastern Rite structure comes from a mountain village known as Tarnawka nad Oporem. (Muzeum Etnograficzne im. Seweryna Udzieli w Krakowie.)

Many Slavs historically have been adherents to Eastern Christianity, including the Eastern Orthodox Church, the Ruthenian (Rusyn, colloquially "Russian") Catholic Church, the Ukrainian Greek Catholic Church, and the Slovak Greek Catholic Church. This 1920 photograph shows Fr. Stefan Korchmowa conducting an Eastern Rite ceremony in Łabowa, a town in the Lemko homeland. (Transfiguration Ukrainian Greek Catholic Church, Shamokin.)

In numerous Slavic cultures, parishioners take baskets to church for blessing during Easter. This practice made its way across the Atlantic Ocean with the original immigrants to the anthracite region and continues today in many ethnic parishes. The photograph shows a basket blessing ceremony in the Old World. Traditionally, participants place a lit candle inside a freshly baked Pascha loaf. (Muzeum Etnograficzne im. Seweryna Udzieli w Krakowie.)

Slavs celebrate a great number of religious feast days throughout the year. Many Eastern Christians have traditionally followed the Julian calendar, with Roman Catholics and other Slavs marking events according to the Gregorian calendar. Frequent processions, such as the one in this photograph, comprised a very popular means for Old World villagers to gather and worship together in celebration of annual church holidays. (Muzeum Etnograficzne im. Seweryna Udzieli w Krakowie.)

While practices varied between groups, all traditional Old World Slavic weddings took place among an intricate host of rituals, beliefs, and superstitions. The time leading up to marriage progressed under the supervision of both sets of parents and occasionally began with the services of a matchmaker and considerable bargaining. After accepting the offer of the groom-to-be, young ladies expressed their desire to wed via numerous means. Some, for example, took great pride in creating an elaborately embroidered shirt for the future husband. Weddings lasted for days, with celebrations taking place in various locations. The photograph above shows a typical Slavic wedding party on horseback. Below, invited guests pose in traditional dress. After arriving into the anthracite region, Slavs continued to hold grand, multiday weddings revolving around time-honored and highly symbolic customs. (Muzeum Etnograficzne im. Seweryna Udzieli w Krakowie.)

Wawel Castle in Krakow, Poland, has always represented a cultural and religious mecca for Poles both at home and abroad. It is to this landmark that the thoughts of Polish immigrants returned to refresh their sense of national pride. Here lie the remains of heroes such as Tadeusz Kosciuszko, Jan Sobieski, Adam Mickiewicz, and St. Stanislaus the Martyr.

In marked contrast to the splendor of Wawel Castle, this type of structure with four-sided thatched roof comprised a common village site in central and eastern Europe during the late 1800s. The exterior of the home helps to illustrate the cult of the Virgin Mary, ubiquitous in Poland, with its shrine on the outside wall facing the camera.

A typical peasant *chata*, or cottage, appears in this photograph. The chata often had a center entrance hallway used for various indoor chores and at times a storage area under the roof. Owners frequently kept their livestock on one side of the hut. Kitchens contained large stoves with areas upon which residents could sleep and stay warm during winter. (Muzeum Etnograficzne im. Seweryna Udzieli w Krakowie; photograph by Roman Reinfuss.)

A common settlement pattern in many villages placed homes nearby each other in a row, with a road or stream in close proximity. Family plots often stretched out on rolling hillsides directly behind the homesteads. This photograph depicts two farms in Smerekowiec, Poland. (Muzeum Etnograficzne im. Seweryna Udzieli w Krakowie; photograph by Jerzy Czajkowski.)

This image shows a cottage in the *powiat* (county) of Ustrzyki Dolne, Poland. In counterbalance to the richly appointed Eastern Christian or Roman Catholic churches found in many rural locations, peasant cottages were simple in design and sparsely decorated. Characteristically, however, they contained icons and other religious articles hanging on interior walls. (Muzeum Etnograficzne im. Seweryna Udzieli w Krakowie; photograph by Roman Reinfuss.)

A large percentage of Slavs entering anthracite towns hailed from rural areas, had worked primarily as farmers in the homeland, and often possessed no knowledge of the mining industry into which they would enter once in the United States. Many of these immigrants came from Austro-Hungarian Galicia and czarist Russia in present-day Poland. This photograph shows a typical rural homestead in Poland during the 19th century. (Polish National Catholic Church.)

While most Slavs arriving into the coal region could be characterized as financially poor, not all families remaining in the homelands fit the stereotype. This photograph was found in a letter sent to the United States from the Old World. The image shows a well-constructed home with tiled roof and concrete walls, standing in relief to the typical wooden and thatched huts of the peasant class. (Polish National Catholic Church.)

This photograph shows a bread vendor and her clients at an outdoor market in Krakow, Poland, then under Austro-Hungarian rule. Krakow lies in the Małopolska region of the country, an area from which many Poles immigrated to the anthracite fields. (Library of Congress, Prints and Photographs Division.)

15661—Bread Market, Cracow, the Ancient Polish Capital, Austria-Hungary.

The Slovak woman in this photograph wears traditional peasant attire. Highly embroidered and ornamental clothing was not for everyday wear; elaborate dress was generally reserved for special occasions such as weddings and holidays. While traditional fashions did make the Atlantic Ocean crossing with the original immigrants, local dress eventually became the norm, especially for United States–born children. (Jankola Library.)

For women, life on a Slavic farm involved a multitude of daily tasks. In addition to their duties around the home, they also toiled in the fields and tended livestock. Part of their chores included raking hay and piling large stacks to be used later as feed. This photograph of two Slavic women was taken in the town of Strubowiska, Poland. (Muzeum Etnograficzne im. Seweryna Udzieli w Krakowie; photograph by Roman Reinfuss.)

As part of their workload, women in Slavic hamlets also performed a variety of traditional textile arts. The woman seen working in this photograph stayed behind in Slovakia as other family members and relatives took up residence in the anthracite region. (Anne Trauger.)

A Slovak girl tends to her infant sibling. Economically depressed times prior to emigration ended unnaturally the childhood of many Slavic youths. Parents put children to work early on, tending to any measure of chores aimed at aiding the family cause. After emigrating, this same work ethic characterized by the needs of the group supplanting those of the individual took firm root in anthracite homes, churches, and secular organizations. (Jankola Library.)

Wash day in a typical Slavic hamlet often took place around a communal spring or other source of freshwater. As the task of tending to animals frequently fell to women and children, it was not unusual to witness scenes similar to the one in this photograph. The picture shows women and children washing clothing at a public well and tending to livestock. (Polish National Catholic Church.)

Life in the homeland was not without its joys and pastimes. In fact, when Slavs began immigrating to coal country, employers repeatedly complained about the large number of holidays celebrated by the new arrivals. Among their popular diversions, Slavs included theater presentations. This image shows an amateur group from Slovakia. As immigration progressed, coal region churches frequently began staging their own theatrical productions in Old World style. (Anne Trauger.)

Two

To America
za Chlebem

In the anthracite region, stories abound of Slavic parents, grandparents, and great-grandparents who left their homes in Europe to establish new lives and families in Pennsylvania. Yet, how often does one consider what a monumental decision it must have been for a young man or woman—who had in many cases previously ventured no farther than a neighboring village—to exchange a centuries-old way of life for what promised to be, at best, an uncertain and risk-filled future? Indeed, for any potential immigrant, the weeks and months leading up to final good-byes likely passed with emotions ranging from excitement and anticipation to absolute fear and consternation.

On departure day, immigrants often said good-bye to younger siblings, perhaps with the hope that they too would someday make their way to the New World. They also bid farewell to parents and extended family members who gazed in silent dismay as one of their own left home—possibly once and for all. Frequently they left their native villages on foot, passing neighbors and familiar sites that they had known since childhood. Many said a prayer in church, asking for blessings and strength. Upon reaching their departure city, some found it nearly unthinkable to set foot on a vessel that threatened to sever permanently all ties with family and region.

Yet they did come to America—and in great numbers. Each person a drop in an enormous wave of immigration that, by the end of the 19th century, thundered headlong onto U.S. shores. After reaching the coal towns, exhausted after weeks of travel, they found little time to rest and quickly came to understand that the real work *za chlebem* (for bread) would only now begin. In most cases, though, they were not alone; in that massive wave reaching as far as the smallest anthracite patch they were to find others like themselves. In a short amount of time, they formed Slavic enclaves and created the nucleus of a culture that would drastically alter the ethnic composition of the anthracite region.

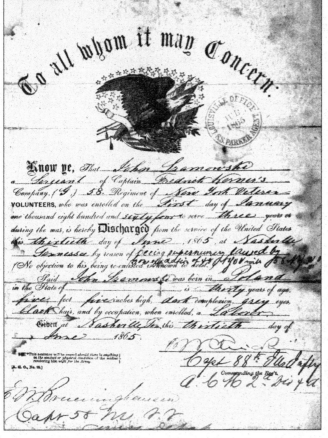

Although relatively few Slavs would immigrate to the region before the 1870s, a few individuals and small groups did indeed begin to place their mark. One such person was John Szumowski, a Pole who came to the area and enlisted into the Union army during the Civil War. While in the military, Szumowski served with the 58th New York Infantry Regiment. Back in his homeland, he also took part in the Crimean War against Russia. This 1893 photograph shows a group of Civil War veterans, including a soldier believed to be Szumowski (back row, second from right, spelled "Szmonski" on the original photograph). Shown in the image at left is Szumowski's discharge paper. His remains currently lie in Holy Trinity Cemetery in Nanticoke. (Above, Nanticoke Historical Society; left, Znaniecki family.)

The year 1868 marks the initial year of Polish colonization in Luzerne County, with Louis Hajdukiewicz constituting the first permanent resident. After that time, Poles began settling in the county, at first in small numbers, then increasingly from the 1880s onward. This 1879 naturalization paper confirms citizenship for a local immigrant born in the part of Poland that had been partitioned and controlled by Russia. (Znaniecki family.)

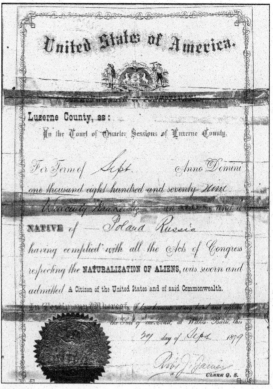

Like Louis Hajdukiewicz and small groups of others before him, John Patrzykowski, seen in this photograph, constituted one of the earlier arrivals when he came to the coal region in 1872. Born in Poland in 1835, he lived during a time of several noted insurrections in his homeland and would have witnessed the abolition of serfdom in Congress Poland in 1864. (Znaniecki family.)

The great immigration to the United States began around 1880, lasting roughly until the mid-1920s. This photograph shows a group of immigrants carrying luggage at perhaps the best-known U.S. entry point, Ellis Island. After passing physical and legal examinations, newly arriving Slavs set off by the thousands to new jobs and places of residence in the anthracite region. (Library of Congress, Prints and Photographs Division; published by Bain News Service.)

With larger numbers of Slavic men generally immigrating before women, many arrivals took photographs to send back home to family members soon after reaching the United States. This picture shows three men who had immigrated to Pennsylvania from Slovakia. (Chuba family.)

32

When husbands had earned sufficient funds to secure travel for any family remaining in the homeland, Slavic wives left for America with young ones by their sides. Upon arrival, they quickly fell into the familiar rhythms of keeping a house, raising a family, and tending to spouses. In this photograph, a woman walks with her children in the Silver Creek, New Philadelphia, area in 1881. (Historical Society of Schuylkill County.)

Unmarried immigrants arriving into the region usually sought partners as soon as feasible. It was most common, indeed expected, for them to find someone within the same ethnic group and to establish a family. Seen here is Andrew Kamenicky and wife Mary, both hailing from eastern Slovakia. Their children, Mary and Anna, were born in Lackawanna County. (Iskra family.)

Commenting on the Slavic family in *The Kingdom of Coal*, Donald L. Miller and Richard E. Sharpless note, "The immigrants transferred family structures intact from the Old World. The family was, above all, a survival mechanism, especially important in the first years of adjustment. The typical family was hierarchical, with the father and older males cast in authority roles, and generally close-knit." This photograph depicts an early family in the Wyoming Valley. (Znaniecki family.)

A common notion depicts Slavic immigrants as largely uneducated and illiterate. On the contrary, many came to the United States already knowing how to read and write in their native language. In *The Slavic Community on Strike*, Victor R. Greene cites a literacy rate of 71 percent among Polish immigrants for a period covering the years 1899–1904. Pictured with a book in this early photograph is a Polish woman in the anthracite region. (Znaniecki family.)

Newly arriving Slavs naturally sought company among their own. Shenandoah quickly became known as a place where immigrants of many different nationalities could find comfort within their individual ethnic group. Here they could speak their native tongue, eat familiar dishes, and generally ease the transition into American life. This photograph shows a rock-strewn Slavic neighborhood in Shenandoah during the year 1891. (Historical Society of Schuylkill County.)

In the anthracite region, the term *patch* still finds frequent use. It refers to small villages historically associated with the mining industry. In the early days of immigration, patches constituted ethnic enclaves and were characterized by roughly constructed housing and generally squalid conditions. This early photograph from Schuylkill County shows a typical coal patch scene. (Historical Society of Schuylkill County.)

The paramilitary group of Poles pictured here reputedly formed in response to threats and ridicule aimed at newly arriving Slavs. When individuals found themselves the victims of jeers and physical attacks at the hands of ethnic groups longer established in the region, the guard allegedly responded in kind with drawn swords and counter activities. Eventually the group curtailed its actions to less-controversial parades and celebrations. (Znaniecki family.)

Although greater attention to church and church life follows in later chapters, it bears mention here that early immigrants sought spiritual guidance upon arriving into the region. In the case of Eastern Christians, priests and their families arrived from the Old World to tend to the needs of the growing ethnic clusters. (Transfiguration Ukrainian Greek Catholic Church, Shamokin.)

As noted in chapter 1, non-Slavic Lithuanians share many cultural and historical commonalities with Poles. As a result, they frequently found themselves grouped together in the minds of many people in the anthracite region. In this photograph from Northumberland County, a group of Lithuanians participate in a patriotic march in Marshallton. (Northumberland County Historical Society.)

Although less numerous than other Slavic groups in the region, Slovenians comprised yet another nationality entering the area. Slovenes hail from southern central Europe and speak a language that is part of the South Slavic group including Serbian, Croatian, and others. In the accompanying photograph from 1905, a Slovenian woman and two children wear their national costume in Forest City. (Forest City News.)

This image comes from a postcard entitled "Homeward Bound." In the photograph, women and children push wheelbarrows filled with coal gathered near a local mine. With very little income, Slavic immigrants found it necessary to make regular trips to area culm banks to pick through discarded materials for bits of anthracite that had not been used by the colliery. (Historical Society of Schuylkill County.)

At times, newly arriving immigrants found their names altered, or transformed completely, in the new land. The family pictured here had an unexpected change of surname upon arrival. Through a misunderstanding, their last name Elias became confused with another term in the native language, an adjectival designation loosely meaning "the one from the street," and the family thereafter became known as the Ulicny family. (Andrew Ulicny.)

Early photographs of immigrant families often reflect the varying degrees of transition and cultural adaptation beginning to take place. In this picture, for example, the knickers, plaid shirt, and baseball cap worn by the young boy stand in striking contrast to the conservative dress and babushkas worn by the mother and oldest girl. (Jankola Library.)

In the early days of immigration, the importance of bars cannot be overstated. Donald L. Miller and Richard E. Sharpless note that they functioned as makeshift hiring halls for laborers, as well as "a place where the immigrant might find temporary lodging, exchange news, find an interpreter or translator or have a letter written." This photograph shows Sedor's in Nanticoke, a town historically with a large Slavic population. (Nanticoke Historical Society.)

In circumstances where one partner in a marriage had passed away, it was not uncommon for an extended family member, or a friend, to fill the void. The man in this first photograph came to the United States from Slovakia. Like many immigrants, he married within his own ethnic group, in this case a woman from Vitez in the homeland. After a few years, the wife passed away in Wilkes-Barre, leaving behind her husband and three young children. Not long after her death, a relative suggested that his own sister in Slovakia would be a suitable partner for the young widower. All concerned agreed to the proposal. This second picture, thus, shows the groom-to-be onboard the USS *Leviathan* returning to the homeland for his new bride. He is accompanied by a group of Slovaks from Luzerne County. (Chuba family.)

Michael Chuba

Three

TO THE MINES

At a time when unfavorable conditions in the homelands placed thoughts of life abroad into the minds of many young Slavs, coal operators on the other side of the Atlantic Ocean found themselves in great need. Ethnic groups that had been longer established in the anthracite region were increasingly reluctant to carry out the most dangerous jobs necessary to extract coal from deep below the surface. The operators, therefore, desired a low-cost and numerically plentiful workforce ready to perform the more hazardous work in the pits. They found their answer in the Slavic people of Europe. In a very short amount of time, colliery owners began working with steamship lines to attract and transport Slavs by the thousands to the anthracite region. The pay was low by American standards but quite high compared to salaries in rural locales in eastern, central, and southern Europe.

From breaker boys to full-fledged miners, Slavs helped build an industry that would, in so many ways, control their lives and ultimately abandon them in times of need. Arriving as young and eager men, many Slavs worked for 30 years or more in the pits before a choking black dust finally snuffed their careers and ended their lives. It was not at all uncommon to find men as young as their mid-40s so stricken with black lung disease that the simple acts of crossing the street or climbing a flight of stairs constituted unachievable tasks.

While Slavic men indeed immigrated to the region to work in a variety of positions outside the collieries, a huge percentage came solely to mine the anthracite coal found locally in great abundance. This brief chapter, therefore, illustrates several aspects of Slavic life in and around the mine site.

In the early coal industry, the positions of miner and laborer were clearly defined. "It was the miner's job to direct the opening and advance of the breast, to cut the coal and prop the roof," state Donald L. Miller and Richard E. Sharpless. Laborers contracted with higher-paid miners, spending many hours loading coal cars long after their bosses had gone home. (Library of Congress, Prints and Photographs Division; published by Bain News Service.)

As newcomers to the trade, Slavic immigrants generally worked as laborers, receiving in the process the most dangerous and lowest-paying jobs in the pits. It was only after a certain amount of time, experience, and, in many cases, luck that they were able to gain miner status. (Forest City News.)

Form 46.—D.

NOTICE TO THE WORKMEN.—You can find out the amount of your earnings at the Office before the tenth day of the month. After that day no errors can be corrected until next month. Sign your name to the receipt below before you come into the Office for your money.

Roll No. *26*

Ticket No. *6*

No. **6 A** Colliery.

EAST NANTICOKE, PA, *June* 188*7*

MR. *Jno. Konitzkie*

In account with SUSQUEHANNA COAL COMPANY.

CR.			DOLLS.	CTS.
By	Yards of Breast,	@		
"	Wagons Coal,	@		
"	Yards Gangway,	@		
"	" Airway,	@		
"	" Heading.	@		
"	" Chute,	@		
"	" Rock Roll,	@		
"	" Bottom,	@		
"	" Timbers,	@		
"	" Top,	@		
"	" Props,	@		
21.6	" Days' Work,	@ *5*	*10*	*80*
	Total Credit,			

DR.				
To Powder,				
" Smithing and Timbers,				
" Labor and Partners,				
" Rent,				
" Coal,				
" Supply Store,			*10*	*72*
" Butcher,				
" Store,				
" Board,				
" Tax,				
" Bridge,				
" Water Rent,				
Total Stoppages,				
Balance Due,				*8*

Many stories describe the great debts owed by mine laborers for goods purchased at company stores, rent for company homes, and so on. This "due bill" from 1887 shows the tally of a Slav named Konitzkie who worked 21.6 days at 50¢ per day, earning a salary of $10.80. After debts were taken into account, the man received a take-home pay of just 8¢. (Znaniecki family.)

It was common practice for early Slavic immigrants to stay in boardinghouses. Frequently owned by fellow countrymen, these homes provided cheap but severely overcrowded accommodations. The woman of the home, usually the owner's wife, did the cooking and cleaning for all the tenants. Additionally, she was responsible for filling bottles of beer as well as washing the backs of workers returning daily from their shifts at the colliery. This photograph from the early 1900s shows a Slovenian housewife, Mary Swegel, scrubbing the back of an unidentified miner, while bottles of beer drawn from the adjacent keg sit on the table. (Ann Shivitz Pavlovich.)

Many immigrants constructed their own coal operations. Often these "bootleg mines" were structurally unstable and resulted in cave-ins and injury. Once a load of anthracite had been extracted at a bootleg site, tipples allowed for easy loading onto trucks. The tipple seen here belonged to a Rusyn immigrant. Independent operations such as this enabled many Slavs to supplement meager incomes and survive financially in their new surroundings. (Emil Simodejka.)

Whether their ethnicity was Slavic, Italian, Welsh, Irish, or any other nationality found in anthracite towns, every resident knew well the site of the local breaker. These deafeningly loud buildings processed coal and broke it into different-size pieces. Workers sometimes referred to the breaker as the "coal cracker." This same term would eventually be used to designate a person who hailed from the region. (Historical Society of Schuylkill County.)

The sense of normalcy conveyed in this 1902 communion picture from St. Mary's (Slovak) church in Shamokin belies the fact that some boys of this age had already begun working for pay. John Dusick (seated, bottom right) would enjoy childhood a year or so longer; however, like many of his young colleagues he would soon begin working in a colliery as a breaker boy separating slate from anthracite. (Dusick family.)

Breaker boys of many nationalities worked at the mine site. Due to sulfur in the coal, they typically developed a skin malady called "red tips," which caused fingers to swell, crack, and bleed. Many also contracted respiratory illnesses from the thick coal dust in the air. This 1911 photograph shows young workers at the Ewen Breaker in South Pittston. (Library of Congress, Prints and Photographs Division; photograph by Lewis Hine.)

After working as breaker boys, many young Slavs went inside the shafts as nippers, spraggers, and mule drivers. As young men, they then became miners' assistants, or laborers, with the ultimate goal of achieving full-fledged miner status while in their physical prime. This photograph shows a group of young Slavic workers in the Wyoming-Lackawanna field. (Znaniecki family.)

Perhaps the most popular mine-related job among Slavic teens was that of mule driver. A July 19, 1885, *New York Times* article states, "In the mines as mule drivers these hardy lads are invaluable. They sing and whistle and laugh and play amid their gloomy surroundings, and they can manage the erratic mule better than most men." This photograph shows a young mule driver exiting a Scranton mine. (Forest City News.)

No text on anthracite Slavs would be complete without the inclusion of non-Slav John Mitchell, onetime president of the United Mine Workers of America. His words "the coal you dig isn't English or Polish or Irish coal, it's coal" rallied ethnic groups throughout the region. In this photograph, Mitchell pays a visit to Shenandoah. (Library of Congress, Prints and Photographs Division.)

On average, Slavic mine workers spent considerably less take-home pay than their counterparts. Nevertheless, payday presented an opportunity for even the most frugal laborer to indulge in an occasional luxury. In order to take advantage of a cash-ready clientele, this local barber offered haircuts and shaves for miners who had just received their wages. (Historical Society of Schuylkill County.)

With time, sacrifice, and prudent saving by household members—including children workers—the typical Slavic family managed to purchase its first home. Often poorly constructed from the cheapest of materials, the house nevertheless represented a large measure of success in the new land. This photograph shows the home of a Polish miner near Scranton in 1912. (Library of Congress, Prints and Photographs Division; published by Bain News Service.)

This 1908 image shows miners at the entrance to a slope in Susquehanna County. By the time of this photograph, the coal industry was in full swing, with Slavs constituting a major portion of the workforce. By 1914, there would be a total of 180,000 people working at local mine sites. (Forest City News.)

Whether blasting in the shafts or processing coal on the surface, it goes without saying that mining has always been an unusually dangerous industry. Accident reports filed over the years present alarming figures of Slavs, Welsh, Irish, Italians, and others killed or injured in the anthracite fields. This photograph shows the aftermath of a breaker accident in Shenandoah in Schuylkill County. (Historical Society of Schuylkill County.)

Mining and industrial accidents contributed to many early adult deaths and created the need for orphanages such as the Jednota Home, founded in 1914 by the First Catholic Slovak Union. Located outside the coal region, this facility nevertheless took in many Slovak children from the area whose parents died at a young age. Pictured here is a group in the orphanage dining hall. (Jankola Library.)

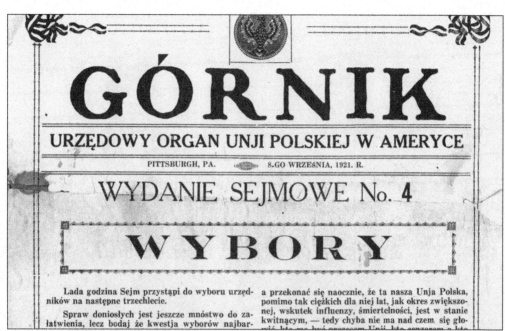

Fraternal organizations filled a key role in the lives of anthracite Slavs. Many formed in answer to the lack of benefits afforded to immigrants by their employers. Organizations such as the Greek Catholic Union, the Polish National Union of America, the Rusyn National Association, the Russian Brotherhood Organization, the First Catholic Slovak Union, the Ladies Pennsylvania Slovak Catholic Union, and others provided benefits to immigrant families. This first image shows a 1921 issue of *Górnik* (the miner), the voice of the Polish Union of America. The second photograph shows a 1929 convention of the Russian Brotherhood Organization (RBO), established in 1900 in Mahanoy City by a group of Carpatho-Rusyns. Like numerous other fraternal societies, the RBO provided death benefits to families who had lost a member as the result of a mining accident. (Above, Polish Union.)

When these Slovak miners posed for a photograph in the 1930s, the anthracite coal industry had already begun to decline. Ongoing labor troubles and a series of strikes in the 1920s and 1930s had taken their toll, as did the rising popularity of oil and gas. Although the industry would continue on for quite some time, production would never again reach its 1917 peak of 100 million tons. (Chuba family.)

Four

ADAPTATION AND EVERYDAY LIFE

Once the Slavic masses had made their way into the cities and towns of the region, they quickly began the processes of adaptation. Initially facing repeated instances of anti-Slav sentiment, they managed to find and keep jobs, save money, build modest homes, and construct churches. With time, they established businesses and eventually won places in local government. They formed social clubs and other secular organizations. They played on or sponsored sports teams. All the while assimilating into the larger fabric of the multiethnic region.

The new generation of Slavs born in the United States attended not only parochial schools but also public educational institutions, where they took part in mainstream learning as well as in extracurricular activities and organizations. At the same time, the older generation strived to encourage and maintain in them a line of continuity leading back to the customs and culture of their native lands. When war came, these same young Slavic Americans showed allegiance to the United States by fighting its cause and, in many cases, offering the supreme sacrifice.

As the original immigrants grew old, they must have viewed their world with a certain sense of loss but also with a feeling of enormous pride. True, they were witnessing a growing, perhaps inevitable, cultural gap between their own experiences back in the homelands and those of their offspring in America. However, as second- and third-generation Slavic Americans began achieving a variety of successes far surpassing their own, they likely felt great satisfaction in knowing that they had laid the cornerstone toward a promising future for their children and grandchildren.

This chapter focuses on adaptation and everyday life. Beginning in a time when the original immigrants had already gained a foothold in the region around the early 20th century, the images show commonplace scenes such as emerging businesses, clubs, musical ensembles, sports teams, and the like. The photographs continue until roughly the late 1950s and early 1960s, long past the "adaptation" stages, and cover what might be described as a sort of golden age of Slavic culture in the area.

In *The Kingdom of Coal*, the authors note a drastic change in the local ethnic composition by the year 1900. When this couple arrived into the region, they were among a tiny minority speaking Slavic languages. "In 1880," the authors state, "English-speaking peoples made up more than 90 percent of the foreign born, but only twenty years later, English speakers were less than 52 percent." (Znaniecki family.)

This photograph shows a Slavic immigrant couple and their children born in the anthracite region. The processes of adaptation and assimilation increasingly came to fruition in first-generation United States–born children. Generally better educated than their parents, they possessed a native understanding of the English language and American culture. With time, they would secure successful positions in business, academia, government, and so on. (John Kameen.)

This photograph shows the main business street in Nanticoke. Historically a hotbed of Slavic culture, this coal town once claimed one of the highest concentrations of Poles per capita in the entire country. (Nanticoke Historical Society.)

By the 20th century, Slavic businesses had become established fixtures in many downtowns throughout the region. Pegalia Rokosz numbered among the proprietors. Along with her sons, Rokosz ran a company selling Voss washing machines. Pictured here are two of the firm's delivery trucks. (Nanticoke Historical Society.)

Felix Dombrowski's jewelry store, established in 1909, constitutes another example of successfully run Slavic businesses that were growing in number. In addition to jewelry, Dombrowski sold sheet music, tobacco, magazines, candy, and religious articles. To supply information to the large Slavic population in Luzerne County, he also sold newspapers in various languages. Pictured from left to right are Zofia Stooks with Dombrowski and his wife Eleonora. (Nanticoke Historical Society.)

While Slavs became successful proprietors of numerous types of specialty shops throughout the area, it was perhaps the neighborhood general store that most locals associate with Slavic business. Neighborhood markets featured daily food items and other essentials. They also, however, sold ethnic fare such as kielbasa and Slavic baked goods. This image shows Baluta's Market in Mount Carmel. (SS. Peter and Paul Ukrainian Catholic Church, Mount Carmel.)

As they gained gradual acceptance from other ethnic groups in the region, increasing allegiance to the United States constitutes a recurring theme among area Slavs. In the first photograph, a local Polish business participates in a patriotic parade on July 4, 1913. In the second image, a group of Poles creates an elaborate float for another local parade in Luzerne County. The theme, "Polish American Division: 1778–1928," celebrates the historical contribution of Poles toward the independence and development of the United States. (In 1778, Congress formally recognized the Pulaski Legion, formed to aid the U.S. cause during the War of Independence). Revolutionary War soldiers lead the float, while commanders appear to make battle plans onboard. Two women stand at the extreme back of the scene, flanked by Polish flags. (Above, Nanticoke Historical Society; below, Polish Union.)

Slavs quickly took up arms in support of the United States during World War I, and years later during World War II as well. This image from 1917 shows a group of army enlistees in the Northern coal field. John Telban, a Slav from Forest City, leads the group and carries an American flag. (Forest City News.)

Polish Americans viewed the outbreak of World War I as an opportunity for their former homeland to regain independence from partitioning powers. The war thus saw many immigrants, now American soldiers, returning to European soil to fight not only for the U.S. cause but also in the hope that Poland would be free by war's end. Included among the Slavic American combatants was Frank Kwiatkowski of Luzerne County, seen here. (Alice Kwiatkowski.)

In many ways Joesph Kamenicky typifies the
first generation of Slavs born in the region.
With one foot firmly planted in American life,
the Jessup native served in the U.S. military
and then later became the town controller and
a successful entrepreneur. He never, however,
overlooked his Slovak heritage. Kamenicky took
an active role in ethnic affairs and presided over
Branch 85 of the First Catholic Slovak Union.
(Iskra family.)

In late 1914, several men of Polish descent were refused membership to a Shenandoah fire
brigade. In response, they formed the Polish American Fire Company in May 1915. Originally
convening in the St. Stanislaus Parochial School, the organization eventually purchased its own
building and remains in operation until today. This photograph shows one of the company's first
trucks, a 1922 American LaFrance pumper. (Polish American Fire Company.)

It has often been said that anthracite coal towns boast a bar or a church on every corner. This Slav ran a Polish drinking club in the anthracite area and, later, two establishments known as the Blue Goose. Maintaining a long-standing coal region tradition, bar owners regularly provided customers with free glasses of beer after several rounds had been purchased.

With names like the Russian Club, the Ukrainian Club, and the Lithuanian Club, drinking establishments throughout the area frequently took on an ethnic character. Seen here are members of the Polish Falcons in Mocanaqua. Ethnically oriented social clubs such as these have traditionally played significant roles as financial supporters of religious and civic activities in anthracite communities. (Polish Falcons Nest 163.)

This photograph from the 1950s shows a Polish Falcons convention for District 7 (northeast Pennsylvania), held at Nest 128 in Duryea. These fraternal "nests" are part of a larger, national network. Polish Falcons in the anthracite coal region today, for example, report to the organization's headquarters in Pittsburgh. (Polish Falcons Nest 163.)

Promoting ethnic culture and physical fitness, area Falcons, or Sokols, historically claimed large memberships and offered activities such as competitive sporting events. This photograph from Luzerne County shows a girls' gymnastics team. The same Sokol that sponsored this group also operated a drum and bugle corps for boys. (Polish Falcons Nest 163.)

In this 1907 photograph, a young man poses in the uniform worn by members of the Polish Sokol. The motto of the organization is *W zdrowym ciele zdrowy duch* (a sound mind in a sound body). (Nanticoke Historical Society.)

Taras Shevchenko (1814–1861) is perhaps the most widely acclaimed Ukrainian poet. He has also been credited for his contribution to the development of the modern Ukrainian language. This Shevchenko Society in Northumberland County was one of a growing number of Slavic secular and religious organizations in the region. In this 1898 picture, the group commemorates the anniversary of the death of the national hero. (Northumberland County Historical Society.)

Once Slavic communities had become firmly established in the United States, secular and religious foreign-language publications soon followed. For example, the Scranton-based National United Women's Societies for the Adoration of the Most Blessed Sacrament served a growing female population with their quarterly *Polka*. In Polish, the term *polka* denotes a Polish woman. Pictured here is the *Polka* staff in 1936. The publication continues into the present. (Polish National Catholic Church.)

Various Slavic organizations throughout the area frequently presented pageants that, in retrospect, clearly illustrated the struggle to maintain ethnic identity while at the same time declare allegiance to all things American. The first photograph depicts a group of young women taking part in a skit entitled "Our Loyalty to Ukraine." In the corresponding picture below, a younger group offers its presentation of "God Bless America." (Transfiguration Ukrainian Greek Catholic Church, Shamokin; photographs by Thomas Photo.)

This photograph comes from a presentation entitled "Ukrainian Folk Ballet: A Pageantry of Historical and Festival Dances," held in November 1935 at the Victoria Theatre in Mount Carmel. New York–based Ivan Zablotsky presented the show featuring local students of ethnic dance. (Northumberland County Historical Society.)

Children belonging to various youth organizations frequently performed at parishes and social events. Presentations often included folk songs, skits, and verses performed in the original language of a given group. In this image, a young boy and girl participate in a show wearing traditional Ukrainian dress. (Transfiguration Ukrainian Greek Catholic Church, Shamokin.)

Slavic youth groups regularly held organized get-togethers for their members. The first photograph shows children participating in a "youth day" in Lackawanna County on July 24, 1938. A picnic, games, songs, and various sporting activities characterized youth days, during which members learned more about their ethnic heritage. In the photograph below from Scranton, a group of young ladies in traditional costume dances at an outdoor get-together to the accompaniment of an accordion. (Polish National Catholic Church.)

As members of cultures steeped in musical tradition, it is no surprise that early Slavic immigrants joined, or formed, local bands after arriving into the area. Dominic Franceski, Frank Franceski, and "Rosey" Franceski are a few of the Slavic members of the Forest City Citizen's Band, seen in this photograph from 1903. (Forest City News.)

The drummer in this 1894 photograph from Shamokin holds a sign in the Cyrillic alphabet that reads "Ruska Banda." The Ruska designation refers here not to the nation state of Russia but rather to the Ruthenian (Rusyn) population from in and near the Carpathian Mountains. As noted earlier, Ruthenians constituted a large portion of immigrants entering the region. (Transfiguration Ukrainian Greek Catholic Church, Shamokin.)

Music accompanied the day-to-day lives of anthracite Slavs. The polka hours on local radio, for example, could regularly be heard streaming up and down the streets of area cities and towns. Here a young boy of Slavic descent plays a toy trumpet along with his great-uncle on harmonica.

The *tamburica* is an instrument most often associated with Slavic folk music from the Balkan Peninsula in southern Europe. Somewhat comparable to a mandolin, it has traditionally enjoyed enormous popularity in Croatia—where it is considered the national instrument—as well as in parts of Serbia and Slovenia. This picture shows a Slovenian tamburica club in Forest City in 1923. (Guy Gerstel.)

Although Slavs were quick to join organized ensembles, it was front porch and backyard get-togethers—such as the informal Slovak gathering here—that highlighted musical expression at the folk level. Participants frequently sang traditional songs and reminisced about life "back home." It was also here that many Slavic American children developed their first awareness of heritage by learning folk tunes brought from the Old World. (Chuba family.)

Whether secular or church-affiliated, choirs constituted a popular pastime for Slavs in the anthracite region. The De Reszke Choir, pictured here, formed in the late 1800s and took its name after two Polish brothers who had gained international fame as operatic singers. Over the years, the choir won numerous prizes at the Assembly of Polish Choirs of America competitions. (Nanticoke Historical Society.)

The Naprej Singing and Dramatic Club poses for this photograph in 1929. *Naprej* is a Slovenian word meaning "forward." It is possible that the group took its name from a well-known Slovenian poem entitled "Naprej zastava slave," meaning "forward, flag of glory!" Slovenians once used this verse as the words for their national anthem. (Barbara Puchnick.)

This early image from 1885 shows a group of Slavic women taking part in an amateur theatrical presentation in Luzerne County. From left to right, they are Celia Kitlowski, "Fillie" Michalowski, and Mary Gronczewski. (Nanticoke Historical Society.)

With time, a large number of folk dance and theater groups began forming throughout the region. Although often associated with ethnic parishes, these troupes were frequently secular in nature. Accompanied by local musicians, they performed a variety of plays and dances. At times, the content consisted of morality tales, such as that of a drunkard or otherwise wayward character. Typically, though, the presentations took a nostalgic, light-hearted look at the past and often revolved around events and themes emanating from the old country. These plays provided local residents with a vehicle to perform the traditional dances and simple songs of their forebears, helping to preserve a culture that was rapidly undergoing major changes *na emigracji*, in immigration. These photographs show two of the many troupes found locally during the first half of the 20th century. (Above, St. Michael's Orthodox Church, Mount Carmel; below, SS. Peter and Paul Ukrainian Catholic Church, Mount Carmel.)

Lansford has historically maintained a very active and diverse Slavic community. Included among the local performing groups in this Carbon County borough was the Slovak *Kružok divadelnych ochotnikov pri osade sv. Michala*, or "the Guild of Theatrical Actors in the Parish of St. Michael." This group called itself Rozmajrin, or "Rosemary." (St. Michael the Archangel Roman Catholic Church, Lansford.)

In this photograph, a Slavic amateur theater group from Kulpmont in Northumberland County poses for a presentation held in May 1931. (Northumberland County Historical Society.)

In addition to providing financial assistance, life insurance, and other fraternal benefits to its members, the Polish National Union of America (PNU) has a long history of sponsoring educational, sporting, and social events. This photograph from the 1930s shows the winner of the PNU's annual beauty pageant. (PNU.)

Long after traditional dress had given way to modern clothing, nostalgia for the past manifested itself in various forms among Slavs throughout the anthracite region. Here a group of Eastern Rite parishioners stages a mock wedding at St. Mary's Greek Catholic Church in Wilkes-Barre. This reenactment of a traditional marriage ceremony took place during the parish sesquicentennial held in 1938. (St. Mary's Greek Catholic Church, Wilkes-Barre.)

In this photograph, two women pose in traditional clothing at a mock wedding in Northumberland County in 1928. Complete with traditional song and dance, these events enjoyed enormous popularity in the 1920s and 1930s. (Olga Coroniti.)

During mock weddings, Slavs reenacted customs and vows associated with the actual ceremonies of a given group. Traditionally, however, they omitted the word *God* when pronouncing the union of man and wife, a union believed to be consecrated only by the Lord. As these events were designed as a festive means to celebrate Old World religion and customs, participants deemed it disrespectful to mock the name of God. (John Kelnock.)

As Slavs entered the mainstream, they naturally began participating in sporting activities beyond those of the primary ethnic group. This photograph from the early 1900s shows the Nanticoke White Sox, a baseball team formed in the area of town known as the "Honey Pot." Members of the squad included Ben Warakomski and Max "the Million Dollar Pitcher" Voshefski, known for his "submarine ball." (Nanticoke Historical Society.)

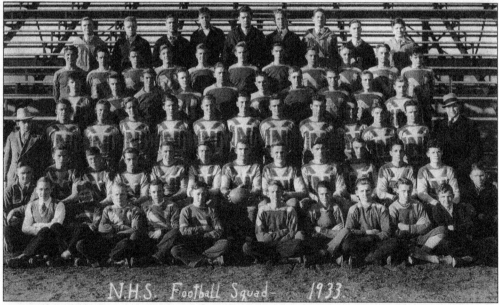

This 1933 photograph of the Nanticoke High School football team illustrates well the mix of ethnicity that had by then taken place in area educational institutions. Alongside player names such as Jones, Ford, Weiss, and Collins appeared the distinctly Slavic names of Bukofski, Shedlosky, Graboski, Kotulak, and Tomporoski, as well as the coach, Frank Chicknoski. (Nanticoke Historical Society.)

The Polish Cadets, a fraternal organization once active in Shamokin, sponsored its own baseball club. In the photograph above, a Cadets batter takes a swing during a game held at the team's home field in the Ferndale section of town. (Joseph Gubernot.)

Women such as those in this last image have served up enormous amounts of ethnic fare over the years at church picnics and ethnic festivals, including *halushki*, *halupki*, *placki*, and pierogi. By the post–World War II period, the large number of Slavic celebrations held throughout the area served as lively reminders of a culture that had successfully integrated American lifestyles with Old World tradition and culture. (Northumberland County Historical Society.)

Five

THE CHURCH

Upon arrival to the towns and cities of the anthracite region, early immigrants often found themselves either unwelcome in or spiritually and linguistically alien to extant religious communities. As a result, they quickly set as a goal the establishment of churches that were closer in line with the spiritual and social milieu of their European homelands.

During the 1870s and 1880s, the anthracite coal region formed a cradle of religious activity for newly founded Slavic parishes in America. Shenandoah witnessed the establishment of the first Ruthenian Greek Catholic Church in the nation. Poles and Lithuanians combined to start their own parishes as well, including St. Stanislaus in Shamokin and St. Casimir's in Shenandoah. Slovak Catholics constructed early churches such as St. Joseph's in Hazleton. Slovak Lutherans also established their own places of worship, beginning with SS. Peter and Paul Lutheran Church, which held its first service in Freeland in 1883.

The church accompanied Slavs at all points in life and arguably functioned on a level equal to family as the most significant unit around which individual energies centered. The importance Slavs placed on their place of worship manifested itself repeatedly in the elaborate and almost cathedral-like designs of many anthracite parishes. As they had done in the old country, even the poorest of immigrants managed to contribute regularly toward their ethnic church and also toward the establishment and maintenance of rectories, convents, seminaries, and schools.

The following two chapters examine the church and parish life, respectively. While the second concentrates on activities and organizations characterizing the typical anthracite Slavic church, the first focuses on the establishment of parishes as institutions and spiritual centers for Slavs in the region. The limited scope of this text precludes a thorough treatment of this rather large topic; neither all churches nor denominations throughout the multicounty coal region receive coverage. Nevertheless, the chapter helps establish an overall picture of the parish and its fundamental role in shaping the Slavic experience in anthracite.

In their desire to build parishes with a distinct ethnic orientation, Slavic nationalities faced a shortage of qualified priests in America. To counter this crisis, they frequently sought clergy in the homelands. This photograph shows a priest on the grounds of a typical small parish in rural Poland. It soon became common practice for European-born pastors such as this to lead flocks in fledgling American churches. (Polish National Catholic Church.)

The Ruthenian population that had been arriving into the anthracite region in the latter half of the 1800s immediately perceived the need to establish churches. Toward that end, Rev. John Wolansky (Volansky) arrived from Europe to aid local residents in founding the first Ruthenian Greek Catholic parish in Shenandoah in 1884. Pictured here is an early image of the first church, dedicated to St. Michael the Archangel. (Pytak family.)

Slovaks entering the area also sought to establish places of worship. In 1882, Fr. Ignatius Jaskovic became pastor of the first church built by Slovak Roman Catholic settlers, St. Joseph's in Hazleton. This drawing shows one of the early church structures, no longer in existence. (St. Joseph's Church, Hazleton, and Jankola Library.)

Members of the rapidly expanding Polish and Lithuanian population in Shamokin desired their own place of worship. Toward that end, they helped found the parish of St. Stanislaus Kosta in 1872, pictured here. Along with St. Casimir's in Shenandoah, these churches were the first parishes of their kind in the state. (Northumberland County Historical Society.)

Under the guidance of local priests such as Fr. Matthew Jankola (1872–1916), Slovak religion and culture began to take root. After the founding of St. Joseph's in Hazleton, other churches quickly followed. This photograph shows the main altar and side altars of St. Michael's, a Slovak Roman Catholic church in Jessup. (Iskra family.)

Francis Hodur, seen here, founded the Polish National Catholic Church in Scranton. Born in Poland, he received his religious education in Krakow and eventually came to the anthracite region in 1893. Perceiving the extensive religious restrictions placed on Poles in the area by longer-established ethnic groups within the church, Hodur formed the Polish National Catholic Church in 1897. (Polish National Catholic Church.)

Similar to the Shenandoah Greek Catholic faithful, the Ruthenian community in and near Shamokin also established a parish in 1884. First holding services in a school and private homes in nearby Excelsior, members ultimately raised funds to construct and dedicate a church building, as yet unnamed, in 1889 (first photograph). Chartered as the Russian Greek Catholic Church in 1896, the parish would undergo a name change in 1913 to the Ruthenian Catholic Church of the Transfiguration of Our Lord. The second photograph, from 1908, shows a new building that eventually replaced the 1889 place of worship. The structure stands until today and functions as Transfiguration Ukrainian Greek Catholic Church. (Transfiguration Ukrainian Greek Catholic Church, Shamokin.)

Ruthenian Church, Shamokin, Pa.   1908

Fr. Matthew Jankola, pictured here, was a noted priest in the early days of Slavic settlement. One of the most influential members of the Slovak diaspora in America, Jankola founded the Sisters of SS. Cyril and Methodius in Scranton in 1909. Throughout his career, Jankola assiduously tended to the spiritual, cultural, and educational needs of Slovaks settling into the region. (Jankola Library.)

In 1890, Slovaks in Carbon County formed a fraternal society aimed at constructing a church in Lansford. They realized this goal one year later with the creation of St. Michael's. After fire destroyed the original building in 1907, workers completed a new structure by 1911. With an original seating capacity of 1,100, the church became known as the "Cathedral in the Coal Region." (St. Michael the Archangel Roman Catholic Church, Lansford.)

In addition to Eastern Rite Catholic churches forming in the area, Orthodox parishes also took root and thrived. Along with their Eastern Catholic counterparts, these congregations built grand, domed structures that were to become an architectural signature for many anthracite cities and villages. This picture shows the construction of St. Michael's Orthodox Church in Mount Carmel, completed in 1908. (St. Michael's Orthodox Church, Mount Carmel.)

Among the Slovaks immigrating to the region were a fair number of Lutherans. Hailing from Zemplin, Zvolen, and other locales in the old country, they banded together after arrival to form parishes in Hazleton, Nanticoke, and Mount Carmel. The year 1899 saw the establishment of St. John the Evangelist Slovak Evangelical Lutheran Church in Lansford. Seen here is the original church building in 1903. (St. John the Evangelist Slovak Evangelical Lutheran Church, Lansford.)

By 1902, Slovenians in Vandling, Browndale, and Forest City numbered around 5,000. To help them found a church of their own, they contacted Bishop Joseph Tomsic, a Slovene stationed in South Dakota. Tomsic acquiesced, as did Bishop Michael J. Hoban of the Scranton Diocese, thus setting the stage for the establishment of St. Joseph's Slovenian Church. Tomsic, seen here, served as the first pastor from 1904 to 1920. (Barbara Puchnick.)

Having established their parish in 1904, members of St. Joseph's congregation immediately sought to construct a church building. With a contracted sum of just under $10,000, work was completed by February 1905. This photograph shows St. Joseph's on its 25th anniversary. The sign above the church doors proclaims, in Slovenian, "Sveti Jozef prosi za nas!" ("St. Joseph pray for us!") (Barbara Puchnick.)

His Excellency Most Reverend Andrew Sheptycky, metropolitan archbishop of Lviv, has long held a special place in ecclesiastical circles. This hierarch, seen on the right, led his flock in the early 20th century. Metropolitan Sheptycky was very influential in the early days of Eastern Rite church development in the United States and was instrumental in securing Soter Ortynsky as the nation's first Ruthenian Catholic bishop. On several occasions, he left eastern Europe to pay visits to followers in North America. In the second photograph, church faithful surround Sheptycky on a 1910 trip to the anthracite coal region. (Right, Transfiguration Ukrainian Greek Catholic Church, Shamokin; below SS. Cyril and Methodius Ukrainian Greek Catholic Church, Olyphant.)

Although Greek Catholic churches began to form in the region in the 1880s, it would be a number of years before the official appointment of a bishop in 1907 to guide the parishes. In this photograph, the first bishop, Soter Ortynsky, blesses the cornerstone of a church in the anthracite region during that same year. (Transfiguration Ukrainian Greek Catholic Church, Shamokin.)

This photograph again shows Bishop Soter Ortynsky. Highly regarded by many, Ortynsky was not without his share of controversy. Factions within the Carpatho-Rusyn community, a group that often advocated a separate identity from Ukraine, resented the bishop for what they felt to be a pro-Ukrainian stance on various matters. (Transfiguration Ukrainian Greek Catholic Church, Shamokin.)

Fr. Jozef Murgaš (1864–1929) came to the United States in 1896 to serve as pastor at Sacred Heart Slovak Church in Wilkes-Barre. As an inventor, painter, botanist, and more, the list of Murgaš's secular achievements arguably places him among the leading intellectuals of his time. The holder of numerous U.S. patents, he pioneered the way in the development of wireless telegraphy and in 1905 successfully conducted a radio transmission between Wilkes-Barre and Scranton. To honor the reverend and his contributions, the U.S. Navy named a ship after him, the SS *Rev. Joseph Murgas* in 1944. In addition to his many secular achievements, Father Murgaš was perhaps most beloved locally for his leadership at Sacred Heart and for his efforts to improve conditions within the Slovak immigrant community. He founded the Slovak Catholic Federation and cofounded the Slovak League of America and the Slovak Catholic Girl's Academy at Villa Sacred Heart. He was also one of the founders of the Congregation Sisters of SS. Cyril and Methodius. (Iskra family.)

With limited finances available to individual parishes, as well as a shortage of pastors to serve the increasing number of faithful, clergymen often split their time between churches. St. John the Evangelist Slovak Evangelical Lutheran Church in Lansford, for example, shared a pastor with congregations in Mahanoy City and Mount Carmel. Ladislav Boor, seen here, became the first official pastor to serve at St. John's. (St. John the Evangelist Slovak Evangelical Lutheran Church.)

The Polish National Catholic Church, having broken with Rome, faced a need to educate and ordain priests to serve the growing population. With this in mind, church administrators established a seminary in Scranton. This photograph shows three young men at the Polish National Catholic Church seminary building on Pittston Street. (Polish National Catholic Church.)

Along with the establishment and maturation of Slavic parishes in the region, a need developed for religious sisters to serve the church community. When Rev. Matthew Jankola founded the Sisters of SS. Cyril and Methodius in Scranton in 1909, he particularly desired that immigrant children received a religious education and that the elderly and impoverished were not forgotten. In this first photograph, three sisters of SS. Cyril and Methodius travel and perform their mission via horse-drawn carriage. Throughout the years, the need for religious sisters of all ethnic groups grew as they increasingly played integral roles in the spiritual and educational life of local Slavic parishes. In the accompanying image from the 1950s, Ukrainian Catholic sisters participate in a groundbreaking ceremony for a new convent in Lackawanna County. (Above, Jankola Library; right, SS. Cyril and Methodius Ukrainian Greek Catholic Church, Olyphant.)

Rich ornamentation behind the main altar, as well as in elaborate adjacent areas venerating the Blessed Virgin Mary and Christ, characterize many Slavic churches in the region. This photograph comes from Holy Ghost Parish (Polish) in Shenandoah, taken in 1932 as the congregation celebrated its 10th anniversary. (Polish National Catholic Church.)

When appointing the interiors of ethnic-based churches, Slavs at times preferred to use religious phrases in the original language rather than the adopted English. For example, the words above the altar in this Lutheran church in Carbon County read, in Slovak, "Glory to God in the highest, and peace and goodwill toward men on earth." (St. John the Evangelist Slovak Evangelical Lutheran Church, Lansford.)

In Eastern Christian churches, the iconostasis is the wall separating the nave from the sanctuary. It traditionally contains three doors, with the center entry referred to as the beautiful gates. A series of religious paintings and icons adorn the wall, each being placed according to prescribed rules and tradition. The top photograph shows the iconostasis from St. Mary's Byzantine Catholic Church in Kingston (established 1887). The second image comes from Transfiguration Ukrainian Greek Catholic Church in Shamokin. Along with several other parishes in the region, these churches number among the earliest examples of Byzantine congregations in the entire nation. (Above, St. Mary's Byzantine Catholic Church, Kingston; below, Transfiguration Ukrainian Greek Catholic Church, Shamokin.)

By the mid-1920s to mid-1930s, some of the early parishes in the region were already celebrating their 50th anniversaries, thus bearing witness to the importance the first Slavic settlers placed on church and church life. The caption in this First Holy Communion photograph reads, in Polish, "The year of the golden anniversary of St. Stanislaus B.M. in Nanticoke, Pa. 1925." (Nanticoke Historical Society.)

With the establishment of ethnic churches, Slavs transported from their native lands institutions offering spiritual guidance and cultural continuity. In many ways, children such as these Polish Americans in Hazleton represented the fruition of early immigrant hopes. Through the efforts of family and church, Slavic youths could participate fully in the American way of life, while retaining religious beliefs and values firmly rooted in distant homelands. (Visitation of the Blessed Virgin Mary Church, Dickson City.)

Six

CHURCH LIFE

It would be difficult to argue that any organization played a more comprehensive role in the lives of Slavic immigrants than did the local church. Once ethnic parishes had been established during the early days of immigration, they provided much more than a simple place to worship; they rapidly became social and educational focal points of day-to-day Slavic life in the region. Organizations such as church choirs, musical bands, women's and men's clubs, prayer groups, and more helped create a syndetic network of ethnic identity, continuity, and support.

For many years, the influence of the church could be seen and heard on nearly every street frequented by Slavs throughout the region. The phrase "Niech bedzie pochwalony Jezus Chrystus" (Let Jesus Christ be praised), to which one replied "Na wieki wieków!" (Forever and ever!), functioned as a daily greeting among Poles. Members of Byzantine Rite parishes proclaimed, "Slava Isusu Christu!" (Glory to Jesus Christ!), with the response of "Slava na v'iki!" (Glory forever!). At the center of these and countless other customs stood the neighborhood church, maintaining as it did a touchstone with traditions transported from the homeland.

While Slavs in the region today have by and large abandoned the religious greetings used by their forebears, many still view the church as an exceptionally important organization in their lives, and a considerable number of parishes continue to maintain a strong ethnic identity. The following chapter examines Slavic parish life, from the early days of settlement until roughly the middle of the 20th century. The images illustrate a few of the many organizations and activities traditionally found in a typical ethnic church and help to demonstrate the great significance—spiritual and social—that Slavs placed on their local place of worship.

Beginning in the early days of settlement, church-related men's groups emerged and grew strong as the Slavic population expanded throughout the region. Membership in parish-sanctioned Ruthenian, Slovak, Polish, Slovene, and other organizations constituted an essential link toward maintaining group solidarity. This photograph shows men belonging to the Towarzystwo Zmartwychwstania (Society of the Resurrection) in Scranton. (Polish National Catholic Church.)

Women, as well, formed many organizations in ethnic parishes, including societies such as the Apostleship of Prayer seen here in Lackawanna County. They also created groups providing financial and physical support to the church, including altar decoration, food preparation, and a host of fund-raising activities. (SS. Cyril and Methodius Ukrainian Greek Catholic Church, Olyphant.)

Lodges frequently maintained a high level of authority and influence over their members. Failure to take part in holy mass or penance regularly, for example, might have resulted in expulsion for men belonging to this group in the Northern coal field. Attendance at the funeral of a lodge member (as seen in this photograph) was also mandatory, with a fine of $1 assessed to those not present. (Barbara Puchnick.)

St. Barbara has long been venerated among Slavs. As the patron saint of mining, she enjoyed enormous popularity in the anthracite area. In 1904, a group of Slavs formed a St. Barbara's Society in the Northern field. Designed to provide aid to miners and their families, the organization grew to national status. Pictured here are members at a 1916 convention in the coal region. (Barbara Puchnick.)

Members of church organizations often wore brightly colored badges and ribbons during processions and other parish-related activities. This photograph shows a badge from the Kostolny Spolok (Church Club) in a local Roman Catholic Slovak parish in 1891. During funerals, members turned the badge on its reverse side, revealing a more somber black cloth, as seen in the second image. (Jankola Library.)

Once ethnically oriented parishes had gained a foothold in the anthracite region, choirs formed to provide support to liturgical events. Singing songs in languages brought from the old country, they quite naturally became organs of cultural and linguistic preservation. In 1894, Fr. John Konstankewicz, a Lemko from the Carpathian Mountains, formed the Boyan Choir pictured in the first photograph at what was then known as the Achoma Greek Catholic Church of Shamokin. The second image shows St. Joseph's Adult Choir (Slovenian) in Forest City in 1912. As with many churches, St. Joseph's also had a children's singing group. Ivan Pregelc (front row, center) served as director of both choirs up until 1914. (Above, Transfiguration Ukrainian Greek Catholic Church, Shamokin; below, Barbara Puchnick.)

Records indicate that as early as 1895 St. Cyril's in Olyphant maintained a chorus that had performed as far as Pittsburgh and had also presented locally its first play, *Znimcheney Yurko*. The group, ultimately numbering around 100 members, gained widespread notoriety and sang at the 1939 New York World's Fair. Performing in English, Ukrainian, and Church Slavonic, the choir continues to the present. (SS. Cyril and Methodius Ukrainian Greek Catholic Church, Olyphant.)

Choirs throughout the region, and at times beyond, occasionally gathered for combined performances or religious services. Wearing traditional clothing, the Ukrainian choirs from Olyphant in Lackawanna County and Sayre in Bradford County assembled for this presentation of traditional music in 1950. (SS. Peter and Paul Ukrainian Catholic Church, Mount Carmel.)

The Ruthenian Band pictured here began in 1914 in Shamokin under the directorship of Anthony Dick and was associated with the Ruthenian Catholic Church of the Transfiguration of Our Lord. The band played at local events until 1930. At that time, Theodore Lubis formed a new band in the parish, called the Ukrainian Band. (Transfiguration Ukrainian Greek Catholic Church, Shamokin.)

In addition to choirs, numerous Slavic churches throughout the region had their own bands. This 1915 photograph shows St. Mary's Band, a Polish group from Nanticoke. This popular marching unit also played for funerals. The caption accompanying the original photograph states that the band "provided the mournful music of muffled drums and mute horns for mourners walking from the church to the cemetery." (Nanticoke Historical Society.)

With Slavic parishes forming in most parts of the coal region, it is only natural that they purchased land to bury church members who had passed away. Local cemeteries still bear witness to the original language and ethnicity of immigrants. This gravestone honors a Polish couple, with the simple words *ojciec* (father) and *matka* (mother), respectively.

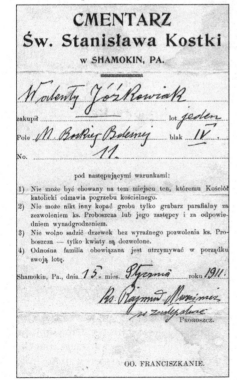

With most early immigrants preferring to speak their native language, church officials often obliged when creating official documents. Seen here is a certificate for the purchase of a cemetery plot. It includes rules regulating the upkeep of the grave site, as well as the stipulation that only the grave digger is allowed to do the digging and that he must be paid an appropriate sum. (Savidge family.)

By the time of these photographs, Slovak, Polish, and Eastern Rite parishes flourished throughout cities and towns in the anthracite region. Large religious ceremonies and gatherings regularly filled churches and parish halls. These included those observing feast days and religious events such as First Holy Communion. This first picture shows children taking part in their First Holy Communion at a Byzantine Rite church in the early 1920s. The second photograph shows a similar group from 1939. These children of Polish descent received their First Holy Communion at the St. Stanislaus Bishop and Martyr Cathedral in Scranton. (Right, St. Nicholas Ukrainian Catholic Church, Minersville; below, Polish National Catholic Church.)

DZIECI PRZYSTĘPUJĄCE DO PIERWSZEJ KOMUNJI ŚW. W KOŚCIELE KATEDRALNYM ŚW. STANISŁAWA B.iM.
W SCRANTON PA. 1szego PAŹDZIERNIKA 1939 ROKU

Tradition in the Roman Catholic Church dictates that children receive their First Holy Communion upon reaching the "age of discretion" (usually around seven years old). This Polish American girl in the anthracite region holds a prayer book, rosary, and candle commemorating the receipt of her first Eucharist. (Chuba family.)

The sacrament of confirmation also comprises another recurring event in parish life. This photograph shows two Roman Catholic Slovenian boys being confirmed in 1913. In contrast to Roman Catholicism, most eastern rites administer confirmation to infants along with baptism. (Barbara Puchnick.)

In addition to events centering on the sacraments, other ceremonies throughout the church year regularly focus Slavs' attention on parish life. During the month of May, for example, many congregations traditionally honor the Blessed Virgin Mary as Mother of God. In this 1948 photograph, a group of young Byzantine Catholic women watch as one of their peers adorns the head of the Virgin with a floral crown. In the second photograph, a younger group poses during a similar ceremony in front of an icon depicting the Virgin Mary and Christ. (Right, St. John the Baptist Byzantine Catholic Church, Hazleton; below, SS. Cyril and Methodius Ukrainian Greek Catholic Church, Olyphant.)

On the whole, early Slavs settling into the anthracite region did not perceive the enrollment of their children into American schools as an immediate priority. In fact, many went so far as to view the public education system as an evil to be avoided at all costs. Donald L. Miller and Richard E. Sharpless note, "Public schools were condemned for their 'antireligious' teachings and emphasis upon materialism and assimilation to 'American' ways. They were seen as places which turned children against their parents and their ethnic heritage." If they were to preserve that which they held culturally dear, therefore, many reasoned that the establishment of a parish school provided the only means toward preserving culture and language while still educating youths in the standard subjects of mathematics, reading, and so on. The parochial school thus emerged as the primary educational route for a large percentage of United States–born Slavs. Pictured here is a 1908 photograph of young children attending a Roman Catholic school in Priceburg. (Visitation of the Blessed Virgin Mary Church, Dickson City.)

In this photograph, Bishop Leon Grochowski (front row, second from left) of the Polish National Catholic Church sits with a group of men known as the Friends of Education Circle in Lackawanna County. In the early days of immigration, men's groups such as this frequently formed to raise money and plan the construction of parish schools. (Polish National Catholic Church.)

The Sisters of SS. Cyril and Methodius, founded in Scranton in 1909, worked alongside local parishes to educate Slovak children. Eventually they established an academy for girls in Danville. This photograph shows three students displaying Slovak American publications in the early days of the school. (Jankola Library.)

RIM. KAT. SLOVENSKÁ ŠKOLA SV. MICHALA ARCHANJELA

JESSUP, PA.

REV. JÁN A. KARNIŠ, DUCHOVNÝ.

Meno *Maria Sporinsky*

Trieda *Ôsma*

Známky 95 do 100 znamenajú výtečne, 90 do 95 vel'mi dobre, 80 do 85 obstojne.

Ked' známky učenia poukazujú niže 75, znamenajú úpadok, preto rodičia sú žiadaní. poradiť sa s učiteľkou, cieľom dosiahnutia lepšieho výsledku v budúcnosti.

Sestry ssv. Cyrilla a Methoda.

As immigrant parents were most comfortable conversing in their native language, this eighth-grade report card from the Roman Catholic School of St. Michael the Archangel in Jessup informs them, in Slovak, of the grading system, as well as of the need for a teacher-parent meeting should student marks fall below 75 percent. (Jankola Library.)

19.. a 19..	Dni vymeškal školu	Vymeškal kostol	Katechismus	Biblia	Slov. mluvnica	Čítanie	Písanie	Kreslenie	Spev	Mravné chovanie	Geography	U. S. History	Grammar	Reading	Spelling	Arithmetic		PODPIS RODIČA
SEPT.			90	90	84	87	90	80	83	95		89	82	88		90	86	
OKT.																		
NOV.																		
DEC.	2		92	73	85	88	92	82	84	95	92	90	90	89	90	92	86	86
JAN.		90	73	84	86				84	9			93	94		94		
FEB.		92	99	98	89	91	95	84	85	99	97	95	96	95	97	96	92	94
MAR.		94	99	98	92	94	96	88	99	100	98	97	98	97	98	97	94	
APR.		96	100	99	94	96	97	90	100	100	99	99	97	98	99	98	96	
MÁJ.		100	99	100	98	100	99	96	100	100	100	100	98	100	84	100	100	
JÚN.																		

Side two of this report card illustrates efforts to educate students in conventional subjects, while simultaneously maintaining Old World connections. Classes taught in Slovak included catechism, reading, writing, singing, and more. English-language subjects seemed geared toward a practical understanding of the adopted culture. Among them were U.S. history, English grammar, geography, and civil government. (Jankola Library.)

With time, Slavs in the anthracite coal region abandoned their initial feelings of mistrust toward American ways and ultimately integrated the concepts of ethnic pride and religion with United States–centered patriotism. In institutions such as this Ukrainian grade school, U.S. flags eventually found their place on walls next to religious paintings and the crucifix. (Transfiguration Ukrainian Greek Catholic Church, Shamokin; photograph by Thomas Photo.)

One important aspect of life in an ethnic parish has historically been the creation of youth organizations that maintain ties with the original culture. These types of organizations hold activities designed to promote ethnic awareness via, for example, music, literature, and art. In this photograph, students learn about and perform traditional dances. (Transfiguration Ukrainian Greek Catholic Church, Shamokin.)

Once Slavs had come to trust and embrace the American system, they encouraged their children to take part in organizations beyond those of their immediate ethnic group. It was not uncommon, therefore, for churches to promote clubs such as local Scouting branches. Seen here are parish-sponsored Boy Scout and Girl Scout troops in Lackawanna County during the 1930s. (SS. Cyril and Methodius Ukrainian Greek Catholic Church, Olyphant.)

Parishes actively maintained numerous organizations for young girls. These often included sodalities formed to pay honor to the Blessed Virgin Mary, as well as groups designed to instill and cultivate social skills and behaviors. The two youth groups shown here come from the parish of SS. Peter and Paul in Mount Carmel. (SS. Peter and Paul Ukrainian Catholic Church, Mount Carmel.)

It would be nearly impossible to estimate the number of pierogi (*pirohi, pyrohy piroshke, varenyky,* and so on) made in the region since the arrival of the first Slavs. This national cuisine has filled homes, restaurants, and church halls in every corner of hard coal country for many decades. At the center of it all in local parishes are the ubiquitous "pierogi ladies." The images of church workers seen here comprise a very familiar sight to nearly anyone growing up in the region. (Above, Polish National Catholic Church; below, SS. Cyril and Methodius Ukrainian Greek Catholic Church, Olyphant.)

Aside from being a culinary mainstay, the making and selling of pierogi has traditionally represented a significant source of income for ethnic parishes and other organizations throughout the region. (Above, SS. Peter and Paul Ukrainian Catholic Church, Mount Carmel; below, Transfiguration Ukrainian Greek Catholic Church, Shamokin.)

Over the years, a large amount of religious-affiliated Slavic sports teams competed throughout the entire region. Seen in this photograph are softball team members of the Young Men's Society of the Resurrection. This long-standing organization continues to hold various fund-raising and recreational events in the area. (Polish National Catholic Church.)

The St. Joseph's Society formed in Forest City in 1893 and soon after became a part of the American Slovenian Catholic Union (KSKJ). For many years, this fraternal organization worked in religious and secular spheres to promote and preserve Slovenian identity in the area. The KSKJ baseball team seen here captured the Tri-County League in 1930. (Barbara Puchnick and Angie Swegel Gliha.)

The young men above played baseball in the early 1940s for the Visitation of the Blessed Virgin Mary Church (Polish) in Dickson City. Led by captain Sylvester (Cy) Kazmerski, the group was one of the best teams ever to emerge from this ethnic parish, counting among its successes championships in the Diamond, International, and County Leagues. Players often met in the school to recite the rosary before games. Girls' teams also enjoyed popularity in the region. The second photograph shows the 1926 girls' basketball squad, also at St. Mary's. Numerous athletes from this parish went on to further sporting achievements, including Joe Glenn, catcher for the New York Yankees, and Jack Koniszewski, who played tackle for the Washington Redskins. (Visitation of the Blessed Virgin Mary Church, Dickson City.)

St. Mary's in Marion Heights also sponsored its own basketball team. This image shows the 1946 squad, a group that captured the championship of the Northern Anthracite League for that year.

Finally, group photographs such as this clearly illustrate the cultural changes that had taken place among Slavic groups by the early 1950s. While maintaining an affiliation with their ethnic heritage through educational and church activities, these boys at St. John the Baptist parochial school nevertheless encapsulate the classic image of American youth during the post–World War II era. (St. John the Baptist Byzantine Catholic Church, Hazleton.)

Seven

TRADITION AND HERITAGE

By the middle of the 20th century, Slavic identity in the anthracite coal region had undergone significant changes. Decades of assimilation and adaptation had drawn the mind-set of the group increasingly away from native European lands. United States–born Slavic Americans identified more strongly with the culture of their own "homeland" than they did with that of their parents or grandparents. Also, the number of original immigrants—the ones with the most enduring connection to the old country—had steadily dwindled. While the children and grandchildren were indeed both Slavic and American, their sense of identity aligned decisively with the latter.

In spite of these factors, however, Slavic Americans did succeed in recognizing and maintaining a great appreciation of their heritage and traditions. While the terms Pole, Ukrainian, Rusyn, Slovak, Slovenian, and so on no longer defined an anthracite resident, they did instill in her or him a sense of ethnic pride, membership, and attachment to a unique group. Even the pejorative expressions once used against Slavs, such as "Hunky," engendered among group members a survivor's sense of distinctiveness and self-regard.

This final chapter looks at Slavic descendants in the region from roughly the 1960s until the present, devoting particular attention to expressions of tradition and heritage. As used here, tradition concerns the observance and maintenance of long-standing customs. This includes, for example, participation in events such as the Slavic Christmas Eve meal (*vilija, wigilia*, and so on) that features traditional foods, well-wishing, and other practices. The second theme, heritage, implies an awareness, expression, and celebration of one's ethnic background. Pride in heritage manifests itself, for example, in membership to a Slavic social club, taking an Easter basket to church for blessing, or learning to make Slavic foods such as poppy seed rolls, "pigeons," and pierogi.

Although the Slavic presence in the area will never be as pervasive as it was in the first half of the 20th century, it still remains quite viable into the present. The following photographs, thus, help to characterize tradition and heritage as understood and practiced by Slavic descendants over the past 50 or so years.

Forest City is unique in the anthracite region due to its relatively heavy concentration of Slovenians. This photograph shows members of a ladies' group, the Slovenian Belles, in national dress as they celebrate their South Slavic heritage during the 1964 centennial celebration held in the town. (Barbara Puchnick.)

Caroling from house to house once constituted an enormously popular holiday custom for area Slavs of all nationalities. Participants dressed in colorful costumes—biblically themed or otherwise imbued with symbolic meaning—including shepherds, wise men, devils, death, angels, and more. Carolers traveled from home to home, such as this local group in the 1970s, receiving money or alcohol in return for songs sung in native Slavic languages. (John Kelnock.)

Slavic baking includes many traditional treats, among them *babka* (an Easter cake), *makowiec* (poppy seed roll), *rogaliki* (croissants with jam filling), and many others. The women seen here have prepared doughnuts, a customary snack eaten by Slavs before Lent on Fat Thursday. On this day, somewhat similar to Fat Tuesday in other cultures, overeating is permitted. (Northumberland County Historical Society; photograph by Thomas Photo.)

Many Slavic homes in the region serve poppy seed rolls or nut rolls during Christmas, Easter, weddings, and other festive occasions. Known by various names, including *makivnyk, horichkovnyk, potica, orechovnik, makowiec,* and more, depending on the nationality, the rolls resemble a type of strudel. Organizations in the region have traditionally baked and sold poppy seed and nut rolls as fund-raisers. (SS. Peter and Paul Ukrainian Catholic Church, Mount Carmel.)

The blessing of Easter baskets has always been a popular tradition among Slavs in the anthracite region. This photograph shows a basket set for blessing in a Ukrainian Catholic church. Typically, contents include eggs, kielbasa, a "butter lamb," Pascha bread (often with a candle inserted), and other ethnic foods covered by an embroidered cloth. (SS. Peter and Paul Ukrainian Catholic Church, Mount Carmel.)

In the 1920s, Slovak American Mary Kamenicky Iskra began taking this basket to church for Easter blessings soon after her marriage. In the 1940s, she received a traditional covering for it from relatives in Slovakia. After she passed away, family members carried on the tradition by using the basket and covering for their own annual Easter blessing, a practice they continue into the present day. (Iskra family.)

Bread plays a significant role in Slavic folk custom. Honored guests, for example, traditionally receive bread and salt as a sign of hospitality. Slavs in the coal region have carried on this centuries-old custom, as seen in this picture from Minersville. Here His Beatitude Myroslav Ivan Cardinal Lubachivsky, former leader of the Ukrainian Greek Catholic Church, receives the traditional gift. (St. Nicholas Ukrainian Catholic Church, Minersville.)

Local Slavic organizations regularly capitalize on the popularity of ethnic foods in the region. In this 2007 photograph, Dr. Peter Yasenchak examines freshly smoked homemade kielbasa, which was later sold to raise money for the Original Byzantine Men's Choir (OBMC) in Minersville. For similar occasions in the past, choir members have made from scratch as much as one ton of the sausage. (Dr. Peter Yasenchak.)

Vladimir (Volodymyr, Volodimir, Valdemar) the Great (around AD 956–1015) ruled Kievan Rus from approximately 980 to 1015. After sending emissaries abroad to representatives of various religions, he accepted Christianity in 988 and made it the official state religion. In 1998, on the 1,000th anniversary of the event, many residents of the coal region celebrated 1,000 years of Ukrainian Christianity, including this group from Lackawanna County. (SS. Cyril and Methodius Ukrainian Greek Catholic Church, Olyphant.)

The story of Centralia in Columbia County has been well documented in various media over the years. With most of its residents now moved to other places due to the long-burning underground mine fire, the town nevertheless still maintains an active Slavic parish. In 2011, Assumption Ukrainian Catholic Church, seen in this photograph, plans to celebrate its 100th anniversary. (SS. Peter and Paul Ukrainian Catholic Church, Mount Carmel.)

Cantors throughout the anthracite area fill the vital role of leading congregations in singing and chanting during Eastern Rite rituals. This photograph from the 1990s shows female cantor Effie Koropchak taking part in a Divine Liturgy. (SS. Peter and Paul Ukrainian Catholic Church, Mount Carmel.)

Numerous theories exist regarding the meaning of the slanted bar on Eastern Christian crosses. One claims that it represents the wood into which Christ's feet were nailed. Another, that Christ lifts the right foot in order to lessen the load of sins for believers. The ornate domes and crosses on local churches bear constant witness to a living faith steeped in eastern European heritage. (Historical Society of Schuylkill County.)

Many families in the coal region continue to observe the Slavic Christmas Eve meal, featuring pierogi, fish, soup, and other meatless dishes. In this photograph, a woman lights a candle in a local ceremony celebrating the event. In Polish, she recites the words "the light of Christ," to which the man replies, "Thanks be to God." (Miscavidge family.)

The OBMC, pictured here, had its beginnings in Schuylkill County in the 1950s. The founding members convened the group with the purpose of preserving traditions and songs brought to the coal region by the original immigrants. As a testament to cultural continuity, OBMC continues to perform into the present with a repertoire of both liturgical and secular music, most often sung in eastern European languages. (Emil Simodejka.)

The Polish Room at Wilkes University houses books, artifacts, and ephemera dedicated to Polish culture and the memory of Polish settlers in the Wyoming Valley. In this photograph, Jules Znaniecki and Stephanie Zimolzak work at a display booth during a local folk festival. The Polish Room, located in the Farley Library, is open to researchers and the public. Those interested may contact the library for more information. (Polish Room, Wilkes University.)

Several of the small fraternal and beneficial societies formed in the early days of immigration have grown tremendously and continue to operate into the present. Among them are the Greek Catholic Union of the U.S.A., the Ukrainian Fraternal Association, and the Russian Brotherhood Organization. Seen here is the June 2008 edition of *Narodna Volya*, the Ukrainian Fraternal Association's official, Scranton-based publication. (Ukrainian Fraternal Association.)

In what has often been called the "Velvet Divorce," Czechoslovakia peacefully split into two nations on January 1, 1993, forming present-day Slovakia and the Czech Republic. In this photograph, Slovaks in Wilkes-Barre commemorate the event in 2002 at the Luzerne County Courthouse. The group holds an annual flag raising to celebrate Slovak heritage. (Iskra family.)

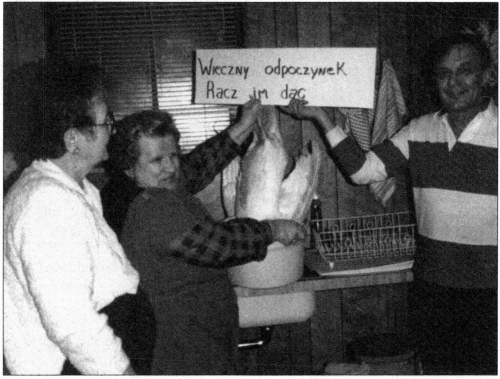

In this photograph, members of the Area Polish Cultural Club in Mount Carmel prepare *zupa z kaczki,* or "duck soup." The inscription held above the duck reads, in Polish, "Grant unto it eternal life." Members of the club continue to meet monthly to cook and sell ethnic food items such as pierogi and *halushki.* (Area Polish Cultural Club.)

Formed in 1983, the Slovak Heritage Society in Wilkes-Barre conducts Slovak-language and cooking classes in the community. It also holds workshops on traditional Easter egg painting, cross-stitch embroidery, choral music, and Slovak dancing. In 2005, its book *Slovak Customs and Traditions* was published in the Slovakian homeland. This photograph shows members of the society dressed in national costume. (Chuba family.)

For many years, polka bands have enjoyed enormous regional popularity. Although they are fewer in number, the groups still play to considerable crowds at church picnics and other events throughout the area. Among the best-known local personalities is John Stanky, leader of Stanky and the Coal Miners. Now well into its sixth decade, the band has released 21 albums. (John Stanky.)

Slavic immigrants brought with them the age-old practice of decorating eggs. Depending on the nationality, the finished egg is known as a *pisanka*, *pysanka*, *kraslica*, or *pisanica*. Pysanky painting continues to be a popular pastime up to the present among many local people with Slavic heritage. In this photograph, three generations of Slavic Americans take lessons at a class held weekly during the Lenten season in 2008.

Local folk artist Rose Demsko, pictured here, has been painting pysanky for over 60 years. The word *pysanka* has a close linguistic correlate to the verb "to write" in various Slavic languages, for example the Ukrainian *pysaty* or the Croat *pisati*. When artists such as Rose Demsko decorate eggs, they "write" their designs in hot wax using a pencil-like stylus.

The Kazka Ukrainian Folk Ensemble, founded in 1987, aims to preserve, promote, and perform traditional music and dance brought to the anthracite region by early immigrants. Kazka remains very active throughout the area and can be seen at events such as this Ukrainian Seminary Day fund-raiser held in July 2008 in Primrose.

This final photograph shows a modern-day mock wedding from Carbon County in 2001. In much the same way that similar gatherings held in the pre–World War II years offered participants a nostalgic look at the past, events such as this offer young Slavs a cultural touchstone with forebears, customs, and tradition. (St. Michael the Archangel Roman Catholic Church, Lansford.)

Visit us at
arcadiapublishing.com

CPSIA information can be obtained
at www.ICGtesting.com
Printed in the USA
BVOW09*1835191216

471259BV00007B/17/P